HOW TO START SEEDS SUCCESSFULLY

Step by step instructions to enable any gardener to confidently produce strong, organic vegetable seedlings that will grow into healthy nourishing food

Ken Bourne

KSB Resources and Publishing Company

FOREST GROVE, BC. Canada

No.1 in the Cariboo Gardener Series

KSB Resources and Publishing Company
4473 Eagle Creek Road,
FOREST GROVE, BC. V0K 1M0

Book Layout © 2017 BookDesignTemplates.com

How to Start Seeds Successfully. Ken Bourne. 1st Edition..

ISBN 978-0-9958805-1-1

This Book is dedicated to the two people who taught me to love gardening. My father, Sid Bourne and my father-in-law Mr. H.G. Bannister

The love of gardening is a seed once sown that never dies.

Gertrude Jeckyll

CONTENTS

INTRODUCTION

Have you ever bought a whole lot of seeds and immediately got down to starting them all right away? Did they all come up and you had thousands of seedlings to transplant, not enough space to put them and many started to keel over and die? Those that survived were either too early or too late to put in your garden so that you had to go to the garden center and buy replacement plants!

Many gardeners have done just that! The tips and tricks you are about to read have been proven to give consistent results. These step by step instructions will give you more insight in starting seeds. You will be able to take control of the process and make your vegetable garden more enjoyable and productive.

How to Start Seeds Successfully is the first of a series of Organic Gardening Books written by Ken Bourne. He has been a very successful organic nurseryman and horticultural consultant for over 50 years. He has had numerous articles published in gardening magazines and was Gardening Correspondent for a local newspaper for over 15 years. He has owned Nurseries, Florists and Garden Centers in the UK and managed a large greenhouse operation in the desert in Abu Dhabi for Sheikh Zayed. For the last 30 years he has operated commercial greenhouses in the interior of British Columbia, Canada, where the climate for growing vegetables creates many problems for gardeners.

This area is called the Cariboo. The name was given it by the gold prospectors who faced the hard winters and difficult conditions in the years of the early gold rush of the late 1850's.

Today this beautiful area is the home of many people who want to escape the negativity of city life and enjoy the many recreation facilities of the area. When they move here, often from more accommodating climates, they are faced with a steep learning curve when it comes to growing a vegetable garden.

However, the local gardeners are very happy to share their knowledge and very soon the newcomers become Cariboo Gardeners who, like the pioneers before them, are able to overcome many obstacles.

This series of books is about gardening under difficult conditions and imparts the knowledge of many Cariboo Gardeners so that gardeners anywhere will be able to grow a healthy, nutritious vegetable garden.

Now retired, the author still operates his nursery where most of the produce is given to local residents and the garden and greenhouse are used to teach organic gardening. He spends most of his spare time giving talks on the benefits of organic gardening, the use of bio-char as a soil additive and sharing his accumulated knowledge by writing this series of gardening books.

Many of the problems that new and experienced gardeners have are at the beginning of the gardening season when they start their seeds. Often they begin the process too early or too late and the results are seldom what they desire.

These problems can be avoided by following a few simple rules that are explained step by step in this book, so that everyone can start their seeds at the right times, give them all the correct conditions and end up harvesting really healthy, tasty and nutritious crops.

CHAPTER ONE

PLANNING YOUR GARDEN

If you are reading this book you are one of many gardeners who want to grow their own vegetables organically and to start their own seeds. What are the benefits of eating organically grown food from your own garden? For a start you will know exactly what went in to the soil to grow your crops. They will taste so much better than shop bought vegetables that have travelled days if not weeks to get on the store shelves. You will have more choice on the type and variety of crops that you grow, and the whole process is much more economical than buying organic food at the supermarket. In my opinion, starting your own seeds and growing your own organic vegetables is like printing your own money. Using the methods of the Cariboo Gardener you will not only learn what to do to get the best tasting and most healthy vegetables and herbs but will also understand the reasons why each step is important.

Why should you start your own seeds instead of buying seedlings from your local garden center? To start with it is cheaper! You can find more varieties in a seed catalogue than are sold at garden centers and you can time the whole production to suit your particular climate and schedule.

Just stopping the use of chemical fertilisers, pesticides and herbicides will in itself not make your garden organic. The soil will have to be rejuvenated. The bacteria and other beneficial living organisms must be replenished and fed a diet that will enable them to extract as many nutrients from the soil as possible to feed your plants. The use of chemicals reduces the amount of beneficial microbes and other helpful living things in your garden, including your best "livestock', worms. Replenishing all of these will make your crops stronger and healthier so that pests and diseases will not be attracted to the weaker and sick plants.

You may already have an organic garden and want to make it more productive and your vegetables even more nutritious. Perhaps you want to convert to organics or maybe you are just starting out and want to create your first garden.

You are going to need a plan, because without one you will not know what seeds you need to sow.

Here are some ideas for your consideration.

If you already have an organic garden, does it supply your family with the food they love to eat? Do you have enough time to look after it? Does the garden need to be enlarged or reduced. Are there other crops that you would like to grow? Can you make or purchase enough compost to keep your garden in perfect condition? Are there some things you need to do to extend the growing season in your area?

If you currently grow with chemicals and want to convert to organics and if you grow your vegetables in rows, you could consider changing to a raised bed system. With raised beds you can grow more and better crops in the same area of garden. I changed to raised beds 45 years ago and have never regretted it! It is far less time consuming and much easier to keep the weeds under control, harvest the crop and you never have to tread on the garden and compact the soil. The soil in raised beds warms up much quicker than that in garden rows. It is also much easier to practice crop rotation with raised beds.

Creating your first vegetable garden is a very exciting and challenging project. Before you come to any decision I would encourage you to start small and as you gain experience increase the size of your garden to suit your ability, your available time and the size of your family. The best place to locate a vegetable garden is on a piece of land with a slope to the South or Southwest. Only you can decide the size of your garden and what crops to produce. Once you have made that decision the next step is to choose the varieties and number of seeds that you will need.

To help you in your decisions here is a list of the approximate yields of a selection of vegetables. The yield is for a 20 foot (6 meters) row. The yield is in Pounds (lbs) with the approximate equivalent in Kilos in brackets. I have also included the amount of seeds or plants needed for this length of row, and the number of persons each row will feed.

Yield for each 20 foot row of vegetables

Asparagus- 6lbs (2.7 kg) 16 crowns will feed 4 persons. Seeds will take 2 years before they are ready to be harvested. One or two year old crowns will obviously be quicker. However I prefer seeds as I get better crops and better spears.

Beans- (Pole) – 30+ lbs (76 kg) Each row needs 3oz (85 g) of seeds and will feed 3-4 persons.

Beans-(Lima)- 4-6 lbs. (2.7 kg kg) Each row needs 3oz (85g) of seeds and will feed 2-3 persons.

Beans (Snap)- 12-20 lbs. (5.4-9 kg) Each row needs 3oz (85g) of seeds and will feed 1-2 persons.

Beet -20 lbs. (9kg) Each row needs 1 packet of seeds and will feed 4 persons.

Broccoli – 16 lbs. (7.2 kg) 16 plants will feed 4 persons.

Cabbage – 40 lbs. (18 kg) 16 plants will feed 4 persons.

Carrot – 20 lbs. (9 kg) each row needs 1 packet of seeds and will feed 2-4 persons.

Corn – 20- 30 ears. One packet of seeds will feed 2 persons.

Cucumber – 20 lbs. (9 kg) one packet of seed will feed 4-6 persons.

Eggplant – 24 lbs. (11kg) 16-plants will feed 4 persons.

Garlic – 8lbs. (3.6 kg) 30 – 40 cloves per row will feed 4-6 persons. In cooler climates like ours it is better if the garlic cloves are planted in the fall.

Lettuce (Leaf)- 14 lbs. (6.3 kg) One packet of seeds will feed 4 persons.

Onion (seed) 14 lbs. (6.3 kg) half of a packet of seeds per row will feed at least 4 persons.

Onion (Sets) 22 lbs. (10 kg) 100 sets will feed 4-6 persons.

Peas (Pod) 12 lbs. (5.4 kg) 3 oz. (85 g) of seeds per row will feed 2 persons.

Peas (shelled) 6 lbs. (2.7 kg) 3 oz. (85 g) of seeds per row will feed 2 persons.

Pepper- 24 lbs. (10.9 kg) 15 plants will feed 2-4 persons.

Potato – 30-60 lbs. (12-27 kg) 20 seed potatoes will feed 2 persons.

Rhubarb – 20-30 lbs.(9-14 kg) A 10 foot row with 6 crowns will feed 2-4 persons. Do not harvest any stalks in the first year and only about 50% in the second.

Spinach - 16 lbs. (7.2 kg) one packet of seeds will feed 4 persons.

Squash (summer)- 50 lbs. (23 kg) one packet of seeds will feed 4 persons.

Squash (winter)- 50 lbs. (23 kg) one packet of seeds will feed 3-4 persons.

Swiss Chard- 20 lbs. (9 kg) one packet of seed will feed 4 persons.

Tomato – 50 lbs. (23 kg) 10 plants will feed 2 persons.

All of the above are estimates. Results will depend on the weather, the soil, and the appetites of the members of your family.

CHAPTER TWO

CHOOSING YOUR SEEDS

Deciding what are the right seeds for your climate, and for you.

Having planned your garden you are in a better position to start deciding what particular seeds you will grow and how many you will need for the upcoming season.

Every place on Earth has its own unique climate zone, and within that zone (your garden) there will be different places where some plants will not thrive and other places where some plants will grow very well. Some parts of your garden will have several hours of sunshine whilst other parts will be in the shade. There might even be micro-climates at the top or bottom of a hill.

The Cariboo Gardener series of books will describe the organic methods used by gardeners to overcome the various problems of growing organic food crops in the climate of the Cariboo region of British Columbia, Canada. However, these same problems are easily overcome in other parts of the World which also have four seasons during the year, or a particular period which is regarded as the optimum growing season, by adjusting the dates given here to suit your particular climate.

The most important aspects of your climate is the length of your growing season, which in North America, and most of Europe, is basically from the last killing frost in the Spring and the first killing frost in the Fall and the average lowest winter temperature. (Over the last 30 years the growing season in North America has increased by up to one week on either end due to climate change. A similar change has also occurred in Europe.)

In this book you will learn step by step how easy it is start your seeds, what containers to grow them in, and the best medium to use to get them germinated. You will also learn how to keep the seedlings healthy and grow them to perfection so that they are ready to be transplanted into your

garden. The timing of starting each variety, giving the right amounts of heat, light, air and water are all covered in this book so that your plants will not become the victims of that dreaded Damping Off disease.

In the Cariboo the growing season can vary from 90 days to 120 days. So the growing period has to be increased by various methods to extend the season. Hence the need to start, or sow some varieties of seeds indoors, plus I find that choosing varieties of seeds that mature early helps to get a head start on the shorter growing season, and sometimes get two crops.

Here is a list of herbs and vegetable seeds that are often started early in the Cariboo:-

HERBS: Basil, Chives, Cilantro, Dill, Various Mints, Parsley, Oregano, Sage, Thyme.

VEGETABLES: Beans (Some beans are better started early, particularly Runner Beans and some bush beans. You can often get two crops of bush beans this way.) Broccoli, Brussels Sprouts, Cabbage, Cauliflower, Celeriac, Celery, Chinese Cabbage, Corn (Sweet Corn), Eggplant, Garlic (I get best results when I plant it in the Fall.) Kohlrabi (this crop needs great care when transplanting!), Leeks, Lettuce, Marrows, Onions, Peppers, Pumpkins, Quinoa (Yes it grows here- I tried it and found it was an easy crop.) Swiss Chard, Tomatoes, Zucchini (Courgettes).

Many of these seeds are started early because some plants do not like the heat of the hot summers here, and sometimes we can get two crops from the same piece of garden, one in the early spring and another in the fall.

Some seed varieties mature earlier than others, so this leaves the space they took when growing available for another crop to take its place.

Not everybody has enough time or space to grow all of these vegetables, so it is very important to plan ahead. Choose only the crops which your family loves to eat and then add a couple of new ones to try, each year.

Knowing the normal start and finish times of your area's growing season, (the period between the last frost in the spring and the first frost in the fall) is critical, as this will help you plan your planting schedule. Check the seed packets or the seed catalogues to find out how many days it takes from sowing the seed to the maturity of each variety that you intend to grow and choose ones that are either quick maturing for early crops or those that need a longer growing period because of the weather.

There are many pests and diseases that can affect most garden plants. Luckily there are now many varieties available that are resistant to many pests and diseases. It will save you much time and anguish if you choose these ones. Also when your garden is organic and you are supplying the correct amounts and mixes of fertilisers and nutrients, you will discover that your plants are

getting more resistant to pests and diseases. This is because the plants are now much stronger and pests and diseases only attack the weaker specimens.

My favorite varieties are Heirloom or Heritage seeds. These varieties have been used and improved over a number of years and saved because of their good taste and reliability. Many of these seeds are available locally at the annual seed swaps of many garden clubs. (See the resources at the end of this book for Seed Companies that specialise in Heirloom and Heritage seeds.) Heirloom seeds are self-pollinating and are not like most hybrids that do not breed true. Some heirloom seeds will cross breed with other similar varieties if they are close enough for the pollinating insects to bring the pollen! These seeds need to be protected from cross pollination if they are grown in the vicinity of other varieties.

I find the best way is to pollinate them yourself. Do this by using a small, soft hair, paint brush and do as the bees do, transfer pollen from one flower to the next. With tomatoes I find that making the strings that hold the ones growing in the greenhouse vibrate at midday does the job really well. To be extra sure you can cover the plants after they have been pollinated with some fleece that is used to protect the plants from insects. If you save the seeds from the best of these plants annually you will be rewarded with your own superb strain of that variety that gets better every year.

Local garden clubs, allotment clubs, community gardens and your neighbors are the best sources to learn which varieties will grow best in your area.

Here is an example of the vegetable and herb seeds that I buy (and save) for our area of the Cariboo. We have only about 90 frost free days (if we are lucky) and the gardening season for planting outside crops starts around the 1st of June, although some hardier vegetables can and should be transplanted and/or sown outside before that date.

Many of the varieties I have decided on this year are early maturing Heritage/Heirloom varieties, plus some non – heirloom varieties that I have grown for decades and are reliable, disease resistant and very tasty! I have saved the seeds of many vegetables for years and now have several unique strains of my own. The days to maturity are in brackets.

HERBS:

Basil. Variety Cinnamon (60-90 Days)

Chives. (I have had the same variety for over 30 years and thin out the plants every 3 years), (80 to 90 days) Once Chives are established they produce all summer and when taken indoors they will produce all winter too!

Cilantro, (60 to 90 days)

Dill. (60 days))

Mints (Various flavors) These herbs are self-seeding and spread on a huge scale! Get a plant from a neighbor and keep it under control by planting it in a container. Use it often as the regular trimming will keep it from getting too leggy.

Parsley (60 days) Parsley needs constant care but is well worth the trouble.

Oregano. Start the seeds 6 to 10 weeks before the last frost and transplant into a large pot if you want to continue to harvest the leaves all winter. (30-50 days from transplants).

Sage. Once transplanted into the garden in the spring you can have dried sage leaves ready for your thanksgiving turkey!

Thyme. Will be harvestable about 60 days from germination- which takes about 2 weeks from sowing in the garden in early Spring.

VEGETABLES:

Beans. (Some beans are better started early, in areas where the growing season is short, particularly Runner Beans (Variety-Scarlet Runner, which is an old English heritage variety) and some bush beans.(The bush bean I use is Provider. This variety was introduced in 1965 and is the earliest maturing bean that I know and is ready to harvest in 50 days) You can often get two crops of bush beans with this one. Harvesting a huge crop is easy if you pick the ripe beans regularly, as they can continue cropping for up to eight weeks.(Mature in 50 days)

Broccoli. Patron (58 days)

Brussels Sprouts. Jade Cross (100 days)

Cabbage. Early Jersey Wakefield (originally from England) (60-70 days from transplants)

Carrots. Touchon - (65-70 days) Scarlet Nantes- (70-75 days)

Cauliflower. Skywalker- (75 days)

Celeriac. Giant Prague celeriac- (110 days)

Celery. Tango- This variety is a hybrid which I grow for the local Fall fairs-(90 days from transplant)

Chinese Cabbage. Emico- (65 days)

Corn (Sweet Corn). Allure-(70 days)

Cucumber. (Slicing)-Raider- (50 days) greenhouse- English telegraph.

Eggplant. Michal- (60-70 days)

Kale. Red Russian. (60 days)

Kohlrabi. Kossack (65 days from transplants)

Leeks. Giant Musselburgh - (100 days)

Lettuce. Edox-(55 days) Paris Island Cos (70-75 days)

Marrows. Cantaloupe- Earlychamp- (85 days)

Okra. Jambalaya- (50-60 days)

Onions, Cortland- (85 days from transplant)

Parsnip. Harris Model- (110-120 days)

Peas. Shell Type- Lincoln-also called Homesteader-60 -65 days) Snap type- Sugar Lace (68 days)

Peppers. Bell type- Tomcat- (75-80 days to red) Hot- Early Jalapeno – (65 days green- 85 days red)

Pumpkin. (This year I was given 2 seeds from the Pumpkin that was the largest grown in BC in 2014 plus the instructions of the methods used by the grower!),

Quinoa (Yes it grows here- I tried it and found it was an easy crop.)

Spinach. Responder- (42 days)

Squash. (summer and winter varieties)-including Spaghetti Squash (Pinnacle- 85 days) Zucchini (Elegance-50 days)

Swiss Chard, Rhubarb and Fordhook Giant- (both mature in about 62 days)

Tomatoes.

My favorite variety is Moneymaker, (I used to grow this variety in my first nursery in England).

I also grow Early Girl and Brandywine, and I regularly try a different variety of the smaller tomatoes which my grandchildren love. They chose Sweet Million which is a hybrid, this year.

Zucchini (Courgettes). Onyx – (50-55 days)

Many gardeners have spent a lot of care and time starting seeds only to have them not germinate, or if they do, to lose the majority of them when they grow spindly and suddenly keel over and die. I think the majority of us gardeners have been in the same situation.

Yes! I have had that happen to me too. Many years ago when I was starting out in my horticultural career my first attempts at seed starting were quite dismal. I blamed the seeds, the soil and anything else that I thought might be the problem!

I was given all sorts of good advice and the most important ones were that you have to have the fresh seeds, clean and sterile containers, a sowing medium that is disease free, (back then everything including soil was sterilised with steam) and to supply adequate heat, light and water.

Chapter Three

PREPARATION

Seed Biology (A simple explanation)

Now that you have scanned the seed catalogues, sent in your order, you have a handful or more, of seed packets. You probably have a few questions like, "Do they need the same conditions or does each variety need different conditions to germinate? In what do I start them? What are the best temperatures? Will they all grow? When is the best time to start them?"

In the packets that you have in your hand are thousands of living things, bursting with energy waiting for you to start them on their exciting life journey. Inside that protective coating is a sleeping, breathing living entity. Yes, a seed breathes in and absorbs oxygen and exhales carbon dioxide through that coat, and they have a built in food store that will keep them alive while they are hibernating and enough for their enzymes to grow the plant into its predestined form.

All that the seeds need are the conditions that will give them a good start on life. The conditions that most seeds require to successfully come out of their hibernation are warmth, darkness, (a few need light) moisture, and air. They do not need any sustenance until they have their first set of true leaves.

Seed Containers

Seeds can be sown or started in containers of many types and shapes. The seed container can be anything that conveniently holds the seed starting mixture, is at least two inches deep, and has drainage holes in the bottom.

These can vary from large plastic seed flats to small peat pellets which expand when wet, plant pots, custom made wooden seed trays, plant tray inserts and the odd plastic containers that were once the home of yogurt, ice cream etc. You can also buy seed starting kits consisting of a seed tray with a rigid clear plastic cover that acts as a mini greenhouse and stops the evaporation of moisture. Whatever container you use you can enclose it in a clear plastic bag and get the same results. My favorite method for small seeds is to use no container at all. What I am talking about are soil blocks.

Soil Blocks

Soil blocks give less shock to the seedlings when they are transplanted into larger containers or into the garden. Transplanting creates some stress in the seedlings as some roots are inevitably damaged in the process. This could put an end to your well laid plans for an early garden as so much time is lost if you have to re-sow a batch of seeds.

Growing your seedlings in soil blocks is the best solution. They are easy to make, inexpensive and really do work. The plants take off immediately because they have a superb root system that has not been damaged by tearing the roots apart.

Soil block machines are available in most garden centers and hardware stores or from many seed companies. The ideal size for the home gardener is one that makes four blocks at a time. Use a seed sowing medium that contains either peat moss or coir (coconut husks), or if you make your own compost, then mix some of that with coarse sand and wet it so that a handful squeezed together retains its shape and does not fall apart.

You fill the four holes of the machine very firmly and depress the lever to eject the four soil blocks. There is a small hole in the top of each block in which you can sow your seeds. For larger seeds just put one seed in the hole. With smaller seeds put in two or three into the hole. When the seeds have germinated reduce them by snipping off the weakest at soil level and leave the strongest plant to mature.

The seedlings in the soil blocks will not need any more fertiliser until they have two to four true leaves and then they can be transplanted. During that time it is very important that the soil blocks are kept quite moist so that they do not fall apart. If kept any longer they can have a weak mixture of compost tea but must be transplanted as soon as their roots start to show through the sides of the sol block.

The second piece of advice that I got from my three mentors was to use a sowing medium that is as sterile as possible, and use clean pots or boxes or containers in which to sow the seeds. If they have been used before, these containers should be clean and sterile.

To do this I use a mixture of 2 parts vinegar to 1 part water. I put this mixture in a spray bottle and spray my seed containers inside and out and then leave it to dry. (I use the empty fly spray bottles we have for our horses. These have the best spray nozzles that last for years.) These bottles are thoroughly cleaned with soap and hot water and some of the vinegar mixture is sprayed through the container to make sure the spray tube is sterile, *before* spraying the seed containers. This will avoid some of the pitfalls that affect newly emerged seedlings, such as, damping off disease.

Damping-Off Disease

Damping-off is the dying of young seedlings at the point where the stems meet the soil. This is mainly caused by parasitic fungi. The fungi live close to the surface of the soil and attack the plant when the growing conditions make it vulnerable. These conditions include, overcrowding of seedlings, lack of aeration in the soil, high humidity, poor air circulation, overwatering and inadequate drainage. You can apply the following remedies; give the plants proper ventilation, dry out the soil and sprinkle powdered charcoal around the plants.

Prevention is far better than a cure! Provide your seed containers with proper drainage. Make sure that there are enough holes in the bottom for drainage. Ensure that your sowing medium is free from unsterilized soil and put the seedlings in a cool, well ventilated position (a small fan works wonders if the air gently blows around the seedlings) and give them plenty of light.

Seed Starting Medium

Seeds need a suitable medium that will hold water and drain well. It should have a consistency that will allow the sprouts to grow into the air and light, and pliable and deep enough for the roots to burrow into and make a solid foundation for the newly emerged plant. Most seeds need darkness to germinate but a few of the smaller ones need light. They should also have enough water and heat to get the process started. What we are aiming to do is to grow a seedling that is as healthy as possible and avoid any conditions that will interrupt its natural development or even cause it to become sick or die.

The medium that your seeds are started in is probably the other most important decision you will make. Do not, under any circumstances, use plain old soil from your garden, unless you have sterilised it first. You can make your own seed starting mixture from easily obtainable products. Here are several recipes that all work well.

Seed Starting Mixture Recipes.

(1) Equal parts (by volume) of Vermiculite, Perlite and Peat moss. These are all natural products except that Peat Moss is not a sustainable substance. You could use Coir as an alternative (it is from coconut husks) but the distance travelled not only makes it expensive but I think the energy used to get it here makes it unsustainable.

(2) Two parts Vermiculite, two parts Perlite, and one part Peat Moss.

Some gardeners use just Peat Moss that has been put through a sieve to make it less coarse and moisten it with warm water.

The John Innes Centre, in the UK, published a various number of formulas in the 1920's for the different stages of plant growth and for different plants. Most gardeners used these religiously for many years, and many still do.

(3) The John Innes formula for Seeds was two parts loam put through a 1/4 inch sieve. Two parts Peat Moss, and one part horticultural sand. (Not the fine builders sand as this easily crusts the surface.) The formula originally included a non-organic fertilizer, superphosphate and also ground chalk (lime). I believe they recommend that the loam is now sterilised.

The seeds only need a medium that will support their roots, hold sufficient water and be coarse enough to allow air in the spaces between the various components. A very simple seed sowing medium with those attributes is all that is required. It does not need any fertilizers.

(4) The formula that I use consists of four ingredients- one part Vermiculite, one part Perlite, one part sterilised garden soil, and one part very fine gravel sand (sometimes called finings) that I pass through a very fine sieve which has 200 holes per square inch.

I get my gravel from the local gravel pit for $20 a cubic yard. This amount gives me at least two years supply for my garden and the oversized leftovers go on my driveway and the paths between my raised beds. The soil I use is the top soil from an area which I do not use for crops. I then sterilise it in a metal container when I make charcoal.

To mix these ingredients I use a 5 gallon bucket and put a bucketful (5 gallons) of each ingredient into a small cement mixer and in 5 minutes it is mixed and ready to go! Another way is to put one gallon of each ingredient into a 5 gallon bucket and then pour the contents into another five gallon bucket. Repeat this four or five times and the result will be the same.

(5) If you cannot get the gravel or any other coarse sand try buying a sterilised seed starting mixture (not potting soil) from your local garden center. You can add equal amounts of Perlite and Vermiculite and that will get you started. If it already has these ingredients then use it without any of these additions.

Sowing Timetable

To decide when to start seedlings indoors in spring, you need to know the approximate date of the last spring frost in your area. Count back from that date the number of weeks indicated below to determine the appropriate starting date for various crops.

Some seedlings, such as leeks, onions, chives and lettuce can be transplanted into the garden 4 weeks before the last frost, as long as the soil is warm enough. (Often the soil is still frozen in our area in mid-April, so we have to wait until the beginning of May before we are able to put these plants in the garden.) Putting black plastic over the soil often warms it up enough to transplant the hardier varieties. Most transplants have to be "hardened off" first so that they do not suffer any setbacks because of the sudden change in temperature.

Hardening off is the process of subjecting the plants for a few hours each day to the cooler temperatures of the garden for about a week. Increase that time over the next week so that they become used to the outdoor environment before they are planted in their permanent positions.

Timing Schedule for individual plants

The first number is the weeks **before** the last frost in your area to sow the seeds indoors and the second is the number of weeks **before** or **after** the last frost to safely set out the seedlings into the garden or the unheated greenhouse. Be ready with some protection if there is danger of frost.

Vegetables

Broccoli- Start indoors 6-8 weeks before last frost- setting out date- up to 4 weeks before last frost. Choose a variety that matures early.

Cabbage- Start 8-10 weeks before- set out up to 4 weeks before, depending on the weather conditions and the condition of the soil. Plant seeds individually in soil blocks and after germination keep the seedlings fairly cool. Transplant the seedlings into 3 or 4 inch pots when the roots show through the sides of the soil block.

Cauliflower- Start 8-10 weeks before- set out up to 4 weeks before, depending on weather and soil conditions. Ensure that the plants do not suffer any setbacks in the early stages of their development as this will result in small or mis-shapen heads.

Cucumber- Start 2-4 weeks before- if the plants are going to be transplanted into the garden - sow 3 seeds in a 4 inch pot- and only water the germinated seedlings from the bottom- choose the strongest seed in each pot and discard the other 2 -repot into a larger pot when the roots reach the bottom of the 4 inch pot.- set out 2-3 weeks after. If the plants are going onto an unheated greenhouse- start the seeds 4-6 weeks before- sow 3 seeds in each 4 inch pot- when germinated choose the strongest and discard the other 2- repot into a 8 inch pot when the roots reach the bottom of the 4 inch pot- do not get any water on the leaves and only water from the bottom. Plant the seedlings in the greenhouse 1 week before last frost.

Eggplant-(Aubergine) start seeds 3 to a 6 inch pot 8-10 weeks before- choose the best seedling in each pot and discard the other 2- if the roots reach the bottom of the 6 inch pot then transplant into a 2 gallon pot- do this carefully as eggplants do not like their roots disturbed- when hardening off the plants keep the roots moist- set out 2-3 weeks after last frost.

Leek- Start 8-10 weeks before- set out in trenches about 6 inches deep, 4 weeks before last frost.

Lettuce- Start 6-8 weeks before- cover seeds very thinly- transplant into 4 inch pots when the seedlings have 2 true leaves and keep the seedlings moist- set out 3 weeks before last frost. To get continuity sow a new crop every two weeks.

Okra- Start 2-4 weeks before- soak the seed for 24 hours to soften the hard coat- sow in deep pots as the taproots are quite long- set out 2-4 weeks after last frost.

Onion- Start 10-12 weeks before- only use new seed- after germination the room temperature should remain below 70 degrees Fahrenheit- set out 2-4 weeks before.

Pepper- Start 4-6 weeks before- put 1 seed in each 4 inch pot- and repot into 1 gallon pots when roots reach the bottom of the 4 inch pot. Do not overwater the seedlings! Set out 1-2 weeks after last frost.

Tomatoes- Start 4-6 weeks before- sow one seed to each 4 inch pot and repot into 1 gallon pots when the roots reach the bottom of the 4 inch pots- set out into garden 2 weeks after the last frost. Transplant into an unheated greenhouse a day or two before the last frost. Tomatoes are quite sensitive to cold, so keep some protection handy to cover them if needed.

CHAPTER FOUR

STARTING THE SEEDS

You have now planned your garden, purchased your seeds and the seed starting mixture. The containers have been selected and sterilised. Now you are ready and confident to start the process of sowing the seeds.

The first thing I do is to place some newspaper (about 2 sheets thick) in the bottom of the container.

This will stop the starting mixture from leaking out of the holes. The paper will allow the mixture to drain.

Pour the mixture into the container until it is within about a quarter inch (8mm) from the top. Do not press it down as this will restrict the roots of the seedlings.

Next put the container into some water which is about 2 inches (5cm) deep. It helps if the water is at room temperature. When the mixture in the container is moist at the top, take it out of the water and leave it to drain.

So now get the first packet of seeds that you are going to start. Read the instructions and open the packet. Most packets of seed will have a small waterproof container in the envelope which protects the seeds until you open it. You can check by testing the envelope with your fingers to feel if it has one. If it does not, then take extra care when you open the packet.

Very carefully pour the seeds into a large spoon. If the seeds are obviously quite large then use a dessert bowl instead.

Now you know the size of the seeds you can start to put them into the mixture in the container. Here is an example of some larger seeds that have been sown in some grooves that were made in the sowing mixture.

If you can pick up a single seed with your fingers then the next step is really easy. I find that broadcasting, or spreading the seeds randomly over the mixture is often very wasteful. You get too many plants and they are often too close together to grow into healthy seedlings.

Make several rows in the top of the container by scratching a shallow groove in the mixture about as deep as three times the diameter of the seed. You can use a pencil, a sharpened piece of wood or even your finger. Most vegetable and herb seeds can be sown an inch apart in these rows. Larger seeds such as cucumber, squash and pumpkin need to be planted singly in a 4 inch (10cm) pot. A few smaller seeds can be picked up between the forefinger and thumb and very carefully deposited along each row by rubbing the thumb against the finger.

Some seeds are very small and difficult to handle so that sowing just a few seeds is almost impossible. One way to get over this problem is to mix some seeds with dry sand. Stir the mixture so that the seeds are distributed throughout the sand and then spread a thin layer of the mixture along each row.

Another trick that I discovered is to put some small seeds on a flat plate or saucer. Then take one sheet of a Post-it note and with the sticky side pick up some of the seeds. With the blade of a pocket knife it is very easy to direct a single seed into the groove in the sowing mixture. This way you can be sure that you have placed the seeds the correct distance apart and not put excess numbers of seeds in different places along the row.

Covering the seeds (or not)

The next step is to cover the seeds. Cover them with your sowing mixture to a depth of about three times the diameter of the seeds. If the seeds are quite large then you use the small mounds of medium that are alongside each row. Use the tool that you used to make the row and drag this down each side to cover the seeds. Then very carefully even out the starting medium using an empty small pot or any flat object. Try to do this very gently as you do not want to compact the mixture as the roots and stems of the new seedlings will have difficulty penetrating it when the seeds have germinated.

The next and very important step is to label the seed container with the variety of the seeds and the date they were sown. More than once I have forgotten when I was sowing several varieties. Over the years I have tried all sorts of ways to cover the smaller seeds and have had the best success, and fewer seedlings dying of damping off disease, if I just put some fine gravel in a sieve with a very fine mesh. I then pass the gravel through the sieve by shaking it from side to side over the newly planted seeds until it reaches the required depth. I just leave this covering as is. The gravel stops any crusting over and the water easily passes through.

Most vegetable seeds do not need light to germinate but there are a few that do. The most important ones are Lettuce and New Zealand spinach. With these seeds sow them on the surface and again very gently press them into the starting mixture and leave them visible so that they have access to the light.

There is another group of vegetable seeds that will germinate with or without light. This group includes the Brassicas (the cabbage family), Cucumber, Squash, Eggplant, Melon, Pepper, and Tomato. I have never tried to grow any of these seeds without light as my results have been fine when they were covered.

Germination

Now we have to make sure that the maximum number of these seeds germinate. To start the germination process all seeds need the soil or medium that they in to be a certain temperature. If you give each variety the optimum temperature the maximum amount of seeds will germinate and they will do that in the shortest time. It is so difficult to be able to provide so many different temperatures that we have to find an average range that will give the best results for most seeds.

Here is list of optimum germination temperatures. The average temperatures range between 65 and 75 degrees F. (18-24 degrees C.) In most houses the average temperature in late winter or

early spring is within that range, so most seeds will germinate successfully. Giving the seeds some additional heat, such as putting the container on top of the fridge or onto a heat mat will help them germinate more quickly.

Vegetable variety	Optimum soil temperature range degrees Celsius	Optimum soil temperature range degrees Fahrenheit	Days to germinate at optimum soil temperature
Beans Lima	30 degrees Celsius	85 degrees F.	7-10 days
Beans snap	24-27 degrees Celsius	75-80 degrees F.	7 days
Beet	24 degrees Celsius	75 degrees F.	7-14 days
Broccoli	18-24 degrees Celsius	65-75 degrees F	5-10 days
Brussels Sprouts	20-24 degrees Celsius	68-75 degrees F.	5-10 days
Cabbage	27-30 degrees Celsius	80-85 degrees F.	5-10 days
Carrot	24 degrees Celsius	75 degrees F.	12-15 days
Cauliflower	18-24 degrees Celsius	65-75 degrees F.	5-10 days
Celery	21-24 degrees Celsius	70-75 degrees F.	10-14 days
Collards	21-24 degrees Celsius	70-75 degrees F.	5-10 days
Corn	24-30 degrees Celsius	75-85 degrees F.	7-10 days
Cucumber	21-30 degrees Celsius	70-85 degrees F.	7-10 days
Eggplant	24-30 degrees Celsius	75-85 degrees F.	10-12 days
Kale	21-24 degrees Celsius	70-75 degrees F.	5-10 days
Kohlrabi	21-24 degrees Celsius	70-75 degrees F.	5-10 days
Lettuce	18-21 degrees Celsius	65-70 degrees F.	7-10 days
Melon	27-30 degrees Celsius	80-85 degrees F.	5-10 days

Okra	27-30 degrees Celsius	80-85 degrees F.	7-14 days
Onions-Bulb	18-24 degrees Celsius	65-75degrees F.	10-14 days
Onions-Bunching	16-21 degrees Celsius	60-70 degrees F.	10-14 days
Parsnip	21 degrees Celsius	70 degrees F.	14-21 days
Pea	18-21 degrees Celsius	65-70 degrees F.	7-14 days
Pepper	26-30 degrees Celsius	78-85 degrees F.	10-14 days
Pumpkin	21-24 degrees Celsius	70-75 degrees F.	7-10 days
Radish	18-21 degrees Celsius	65-70 degrees F.	5-7 days
Rutabaga	18-21 degrees Celsius	65-70 degrees F.	7-15 days
Spinach	21 degrees Celsius	70 degrees	7-14 days
Spinach NZ	24 degrees Celsius	75 degrees F.	10-15 days
Squash-Summer	24-30 degrees Celsius	75-85 degrees F.	7-14 days
Squash-Winter	24-27 degrees Celsius	75-80 degrees F.	7-14 days
Swiss Chard	21-24 degrees Celsius	70-75 degrees F.	7-14 days
Tomato	24-27 degrees Celsius	75-80 degrees F.	7-14 days
Turnip	18-21 degrees Celsius	65-70 degrees F.	7-14 days

Seeds need water to penetrate their shell so that they will be able to begin the germination process. Although they were planted into the moist medium they now need to be thoroughly moistened by gently spraying them with tepid or lukewarm water.

To stop the seeds from drying out cover the container with cardboard and then put it into a plastic bag, or, if you have a seed starting kit just put the rigid cover over the seed tray . Whatever cover you use remove it once a day to check that the seed mixture is still moist, but not too wet.

As seedlings must never dry out I spray each container with tepid water whenever the surface of the seedling mix starts to dry out. As soon as the seeds germinate you can remove the cover completely and then only water the containers from the bottom.

The Seedlings' First Feed.

Now that your seeds have germinated the new seedlings will need special care so that they develop into strong, healthy, compact plants.

When the seedlings have developed their first set of true leaves they will have exhausted most of the nutrients that were in the embryo and will need a feed to keep them growing.

I give them their first feed of a diluted mixture of liquid seaweed (kelp), watered down to about a quarter of the amount as directed by the instructions on the container. The first feed I spray onto the leaves and around the roots of the seedlings.

If you are using tap water that has been treated with fluoride and/or chloride put some into a suitable container and let it stand for about 48 hours before using i

. Remember never to use water straight from the tap as it is too cold and could check the growth of the seedlings.

The seedlings should be moved to an area away from the heat source as they now do not need as much heat.

In fact 10 degrees cooler will give you much stronger, compact and healthier plants

Light

This new area should enable the seedlings to get as much sunlight as possible. A sunny, south facing window in the house or in a heated greenhouse often works, but fluorescent light tubes will supply your plants with the right amount of light to get the best results.

It is important to keep the fluorescent lights about 3 inches (7.5 cm.) above the leaves of the seedlings. As the seedlings grow adjust the height appropriately.

The time that the lights are on is also important. I find that 16 hours a day gives very good results.

Buying a light stand can be very expensive but making your own is relatively easy and inexpensive.

I normally start all my seeds in the greenhouse, however this year there was so much snow that I decided to start some in the our house. Our house is oriented from North to South so the sun is on the east windows in the morning and the west windows in the afternoon.

Consequently I had to make a light stand.

Luckily I had everything that was needed in my workshop. I used three shop lights (each one had two 4 foot fluorescent tubes) and made the frame from some 2X4's that I sawed in half, length ways.

For the shelves I used an old piece of OSB (strand board). To buy the same things from a store would cost about $60 Canadian, compared to the price of a similar light stand from the local gardening store of over $500!

Mine is not pretty but it does the job. The first seedlings I tried in it got a little leggy at first until I adjusted the height of the lights so that they were much closer to the seedlings.

As the seedlings grew I increased the distance from them moved the lights higher but kept them close to the top of the seedlings. I was very pleased with results and the photo shows how healthy the seedlings were.

Transplanting the Seedlings

When the seedlings produce their first set of true leaves they will need to be transplanted so that they will not be competing with the other plants for light and food and their roots will have more room to grow. These Cilantro seedlings are ready to be transplanted

Step 1.

Choose the size of container that you are going to use. For the majority of transplants the inserts that go into seed trays work very well. (I used one in the following photos.) The larger seeds such as tomatoes, squashes and cucumbers will have been started in their own individual pots, so they will need a size larger pot as soon as their roots reach the bottom of their starter pot.

Fill the container loosely with moist potting soil. I always use a new supply each year as most of my transplanting is done in late winter or very early spring. At those times our soil is frozen so that I cannot get any of my own soil and I can rely on the bought mixture to be free of diseases.

Most potting soils contain a certain amount of fertilizer but this is often not sufficient. I give all of the newly transplanted seedlings a weekly foliar spray of liquid seaweed (Kelp) and liquid fish fertilizer. (This is mixed with water at half the recommended rate.)

When the container is full, gently press the mixture down so that it is about a quarter inch (6mm) from the top. Using the bottom of a similar sized container works really well.

Step 2.

Very carefully dig around some seedlings with a spoon or a dibber, to separate them from the seed mixture. Try to disturb the roots as little as possible. Collect about 12 seedlings and place them in a small container. Cover the roots with Willow Root booster.

Willow trees contain hormones that stimulate root growth. This method of ensuring rapid root development was passed down to me by my grandfather, over 50 years ago. He was a charcoal burner and also had several coppices in Sussex, England. Stick a twig of willow in the soil and very soon you will see leaves growing! Willow Root Booster is made by extracting these hormones.

In the early spring, when the sap in the trees starts to flow, collect a few branches of Willow (any variety) which are about ½ inch (12mm) thick. Cut these into 1 inch (24mm.) lengths. Put a handful of these pieces into a litre of boiling water. Let the water cool and leave the pieces of willow in it for 24 hours. You now have some Willow Root Booster. You can use this mixture

for transplanting, taking cuttings and as an extra feed for your root vegetables. I find that it works best when it is not more than 3 days old. You can keep it in the fridge for 3 days.

Leave the seedlings in the Willow Root Booster for 1 hour.

Step 3.

Now you can transplant the seedlings. Pick up each seedling by holding a leaf between the thumb and forefinger. Avoid touching the stem as it is very delicate as if it is damaged the seedling will not grow properly.

With the dibber (a dibber is shown in the above photo- it is a small, blunt twig that has two sides flattened.) or even a blunt pencil, make a hole in the potting soil in the container. Make the hole a little deeper than the seedling was originally. Carefully place the seedling in hole, ensuring that the roots are all at the bottom and not twisted or damaged. Then gently firm the soil around the stem. I do this with my fingers. Plant each seedling at least 2 inches away from its neighbors. This will give their roots space to grow and not compete for water and nutrients.

Step 4

Now place the transplanted seedlings where they will get as much sunlight as possible, or put them on your newly made light shelves. Give them their first feed and watering, from the bottom. Put the seedling tray or pot into a container that has about 2 inches (5cm) of water to which has been added liquid fish and seaweed (kelp) fertilizer at half the recommended strength. Leave it in there for about 20 minutes or until you can see that the surface of the potting soil is moist.

Now that the seedlings have been transplanted they will need special care over the next few weeks. They need to grow and produce strong stems and roots. The potting soil must never be allowed to dry out.

I find the best way to check is by the weight of the container. Fill a similar one with fairly dry potting soil. Pick it up and feel the weight. Do this several times. Then water the soil until the top is moist. Pick this up and you will immediately feel the difference. Every day it is easy to check the containers to see if they need water.

Once a week, until the seedlings are put into the garden or the greenhouse, feed them with a full strength mixture of fish and seaweed fertilizer.

The seedlings will grow much stronger if there is a fan close to them so that the air is changed around them often. The fan should not blow directly towards them but just enough to make the leaves and stems gently move.

If the seedlings get their light from a window you will notice that they bend towards the light. Turn the containers around so that they face in the opposite direction, once a day. This will keep the seedlings growing as straight as possible.

So far we have covered the essentials of starting seeds indoors.

You have-planned your garden-chosen the seeds, containers and the sowing medium -made a schedule and started your seeds. -transplanted and cared for the seedlings until they are ready to be put into your garden, where they will grow with the other seeds you are about to start.

Chapter Five

PREPARING THE GARDEN SOIL

Transplanting the Seedlings and sowing Seeds directly into the Garden

There are a few things that need to be done before you transplant seedlings or sow seeds directly into the garden.

The very first thing is to make sure that the soil is not wet. If you walk on or even disturb the soil when it is wet it can cause almost irreparable damage. Wait until the soil is dry enough and then take a soil sample and have the soil tested so that you know exactly how much fertilizer you need to put on. The nominal cost of about $20 is worth every penny! Then check the temperature and the pH of the soil. A soil thermometer and a pH meter are two garden tools that enable you to transplant the seedlings or sow the seeds at the correct soil temperature and ensure that the soil has the correct pH. This will allow the plant's roots to extract the maximum number of nutrients from the soil. You will know that these nutrients are there to be extracted if you have a soil test done!

Testing the Soil

Whether you are just starting a new garden, rebuilding an old one or preparing to grow your crops in your existing garden knowing how much fertilizer and nutrients are in your soil is particularly important. If you have not had the soil tested in a laboratory I would advise you to get one as soon as possible.

You can get a soil testing kit from most garden centers and hardware stores, but the results are normally not very specific and only deal with Nitrogen, Phosphate and Potassium. What is needed is a detailed report on the state of the available fertilisers in your soil, plus the amount of magnesium. Only a reputable laboratory can do this. A soil test will not only save you money but will enable you to put in only the required fertilisers that will boost the vigor, health and taste of your crops.

Every country has different rules for soil testing. Each laboratory will supply details of their requirements and often send a kit with full instructions on how to take a soil sample.

Here is a list of laboratories where you can get your soil tested in various parts of the world.

In Canada- the following website has a detailed list of Laboratories for each province and territory- http://www.agf.gov.bc.ca/faq

In the UK-

http://www.angliansoil.co.uk   phone 01205 460 590

www.soilassociation.org

www.eurofins.co.uk

www.laverstokepark.co.uk/soil_testing_laboratory

In Australia-

There are many soil testing laboratories that do soil testing. I have put a list in the **Resources** section at the back of this book.

In the USA-

Each state has laboratories at the State Agricultural Experiment Station or Extension service where soil tests are conducted. I also have included a list of private soil testing Companies in the **Resources** section at the back of this book. These are more expensive than the Experiment Stations or Extension services but they can give you more in depth results. Some will even give you recommendations on the amount of Organic fertilizer to put on your garden.

The Test and Results

Wherever you get the results from, the laboratory will give you instructions on how much fertilizer to put on your garden. The most difficult thing for a lot of organic gardeners is converting the weights of chemical fertilizers to the equivalent organic weights.

To avoid these problems choose a company that will conduct your soil test and give you the results and recommendations in organic equivalents. Many companies will do this and for a fee will include results on micronutrients as well.

They will also tell you the pH of the soil, and how much Magnesium is needed if any.

There is a link to a sample soil test and recommendations in this book's **Resources** section. **These links may be a problem to copy as well as the links in the Resources, so I have a PDF file on my website that you can download to your computer or cell phone. The link to my site is, www.cariboogardener.com/pdf.**

Apply the appropriate amounts evenly to garden and fork them in about 6 inch deep (15cm) so that the fertilizers are thoroughly mixed with the soil.

If you decide not to have a soil test because of time restrictions or any other reason there is an alternative. You can add a "complete organic fertilizer" to your soil. This will enable you to harvest a good crop the first year without too many problems. The formula that I am about to give you will feed your whole garden for one growing season and leave the garden after harvest with about the same nutrients that were there before the fertilizer was added. It would be a good thing to get your soil test done then so that you can adjust the soil for the following year.

I get a soil test done every 4 years and follow the instructions to adjust my garden soil for that year. After that I use the following complete organic fertilizer each year for three years, or earlier if my yields start to fluctuate.

I have had my own formula for several years but changed it slightly after reading "The Intelligent Gardener", a superb gardening book about growing nutrient dense food, written by Steve Solomon with Erica Reinheimer.

Steve Solomon's formula is basically for any garden and is adjustable for different areas. My own soil is very sandy with very little organic matter, so I have had to add enormous amounts of compost over the 30 years that I have lived here. This improved considerably when I changed over completely from rows to raised beds. I also made slight changes to his formula that so far has made my garden much more prolific.

Complete Organic Fertilizer Formula.

11/2 liters feathermeal

1 liter bonemeal

1 liter kelp meal

½ liter lime

½ liter gypsum

½ teaspoon Borax

Mix all the ingredients together and the resulting mixture will be sufficient for 100 square feet (9.29 square meters) of garden.

It is very important that the small amount of Borax is thoroughly mixed with the other ingredients so that it is evenly distributed throughout the garden. The soil only needs a maximum of 3 parts per billion of Boron. Plants need boron to transport nutrients between the plant and the bacteria in the soil and to create a stronger cell structure. However too much Boron will have a negative effect!

Put this fertilizer on the garden about 4 weeks before planting out your seedlings. If you are unable to add it this early then put it on your garden as soon as possible. Add about an inch (2 or 3 cm) of compost on the fertilizer and then fork the mixture into the top 4-6 inches (10-15 cm) of the topsoil.

Ideal Soil Temperatures for Transplanting and Sowing Seeds

Each variety of vegetables has an optimum soil temperature to enable the seeds to germinate and the transplanted seedlings to grow strong roots. Here is list of the minimum temperatures required by each variety for sowing seeds or transplanting the seedlings. I have also included the optimum range of temperatures that will give the best results.

Vegetables

Asparagus-Min. 50 deg. F (10 deg. C)—optimum range-60-85 deg. F (15-30 deg. C)

Bean.-Min. 60 deg. F (15 deg. C)—optimum range-60-85 deg. F (15-30 deg. C)

Bean, Lima-Min.60 deg. F (15 deg. C)--optimum range-65-85 deg. F (18-30 deg. C)

Beet –Min. 40 deg. F (5 deg. C)—optimum range-50-95 deg. F (10-35 deg. C)

Cabbage.-Min. 40 deg. F (5 deg. C—optimum range-45-85 deg. F (8-30 deg. C)

Carrot.-Min. 40 deg. F (5 deg. C) ---optimum range-45-85 deg. F (8-30 deg. C)

Cauliflower.-Min. 40 deg. F (5 deg. C) ---optimum range-45-85 deg. F (8-30 deg. C)

Celery.-Min. 40 deg. F (5 deg. C) ---optimum range-60-70 deg. F (15-22 deg. C)

Chard, Swiss.-Min. 40 deg. F (5 deg. C) ---optimum range-50-85 deg. F (10-30 deg. C)

Corn.-Min. 50 deg. F (10 deg. C) ---optimum range-60-95 deg. F (15-35 deg. C)

Cucumber -Min. 60 deg. F (15 deg. C) ---optimum range-60-95 deg. F (15-35 deg. C)

Eggplant –Min. 35 deg. F (3 deg. C) ---optimum range-75-90 deg. F (24-33 deg. C)

Lettuce –Min. 35 deg. F (3 deg. C) ---optimum range-40-80- deg. F (5-27 deg. C)

Okra –Min. 60 deg. F (15 deg. C) ---optimum range-70-95 deg. F (22-35 deg. C)

Onion –Min. 35 deg. F (3 deg. C) ---optimum range-50-95 deg. F (10 -35 deg. C)

Parsley –Min. 40 deg. F (5 deg. C) ---optimum range- 50-85 deg. F (10-30 deg. C)

Parsnip –Min. 35 deg. F (3 deg. C) ---optimum range-50-70 deg. F (10-22 deg. C)

Pea –Min. 40 deg. F (5 deg. C) ---optimum range-40-75 deg. F (5-24 deg. C)

Pepper –Min. 60 deg. F (25 deg. C) ---optimum range-65-95 deg. F (18-35 deg. C)

Pumpkin –Min. 60 deg. F (25 deg. C) ---optimum range-70-90 deg. F (22-33 deg. C)

Radish –Min. 40 deg. F (5 deg. C) ---optimum range- 45-90 deg. F (8-33 deg. C)

Spinach –Min. 35 deg. F (3 deg. C) ---optimum range-45-75 deg. F (8-24 deg. C)

Squash –Min. 60 deg. F (25 deg. C) ---optimum range 70-95 deg. F (22-33 deg. C)

Tomato –Min. 50 deg. F (10 deg. C) ---optimum range-70-95 deg. F (22-33 deg. C)

Turnip –Min. 40 deg. F (5 deg. C) ---optimum range-60-100 deg. F (15-37 deg. C)

As you can see from the above list, there is such a range of optimum temperatures that it is impossible to have them all at one time.

There is a temperature between the minimum and optimum temperatures that will allow the transplants to grow and the seeds to germinate. I call this the realistic temperature.

The vegetables can be divided into three groups. The first group is the ones that grow best in the colder temperatures of early spring.

The vegetables in this group are; Asparagus, Beets, Cabbage, Carrots, Cauliflower, Celery, Chard (Swiss), Lettuce, Onion, Parsley, Parsnip, Pea, Radish, Spinach, Turnip. You can safely transplant or start the seeds of these varieties when the soil temperature is at 45 degrees F. (8deg.C). This is the realistic temperature.

The second group consists of those vegetables that tolerate cooler soil temperatures. These are Beans, Corn, Eggplant, Pepper and Tomato.

The realistic temperature for this group is 50- 65 degrees F. (10-18 degrees C).

The third group needs warmer soil temperatures to enable them to grow to perfection. They are Cucumber, Okra, Pumpkin and Squash.

Their realistic soil temperature is 70 degrees F. (22 degrees C).

Testing the Soil Temperature.

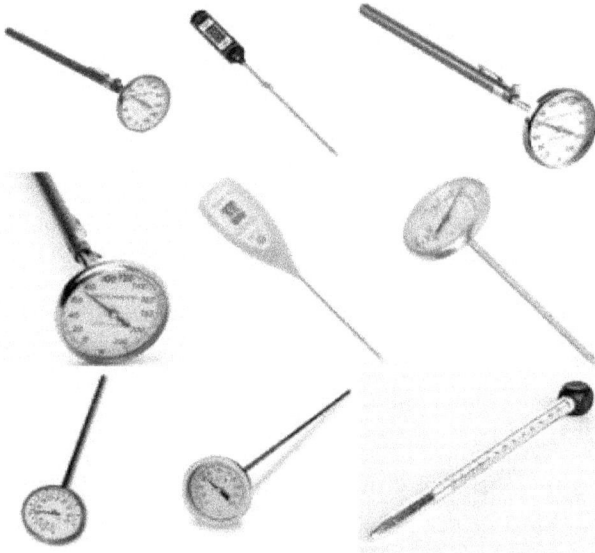

It is well worth buying a soil thermometer! There are many types available and the current prices vary between $9 and $30. The one that I use has a dial at the top and the temperature scale is in both F. and C. It also gives a reading in about a minute and so far, after 6 years, has not been damaged by accidentally dropping it onto the concrete path or by digging it up with the fork. It had been left in the soil by my granddaughter when she was 'helping' me plant some seedlings. And no, I do not test the temperature of the soil by sitting on it to see whether it is comfortable to my bare skin. This was something my grandfather said was the best way! He always had a great garden but to my knowledge no one ever saw him test the temperature of his soil that way!

How to Test the Soil Temperature

Make a pilot hole for your thermometer with a screwdriver, and loosen the soil at the bottom of the hole. This will avoid breaking the delicate thermometer if you push it into very hard soil.

If you are transplanting make the hole about 6 inches (15 cm.) deep as the roots will soon reach this depth after the seedlings have been planted. For seeds a depth of 4 inches (10 cm.) is sufficient as the seeds will not germinate for a while and the soil will gradually heat up any way.

Read the directions that came with the thermometer. Place the thermometer in the hole with the bulb in the loose soil at the bottom. Wait a couple of minutes and then check and record the temperature. Do this in several places where you intend to either transplant seedlings or start some seeds. You can now work out the average temperature of the soil.

Your next task is to check the pH of the soil. This is just as important as the temperature. The pH measures the acidity or alkalinity of the soil. There is a scale which runs from 1 to 14. Number 1 on the scale is very acid and number 14 is very alkaline. The number 7 is where the soil is neither acid nor alkaline. Pure water has a pH of 7.

A pH measurement which is too low or too high restricts the roots of the plants from taking up certain nutrients. Most plants will do just fine when the pH is between 6.4 and 6.9. That is slightly acid. Potatoes prefer the soil to be even more acid, a pH of 6 will work for them.

How to test the pH of the soil.

You will need another inexpensive tool to do this. I use the one in the photo below. It measures the pH and also the fertility of the soil. (However I prefer to test the soil fertility once a year with a kit I purchased and every three years I get the soil tested again by sending a sample to the Ministry of Agriculture.)

Testing the soil pH is really easy.

As soon as you can safely get into your garden in the spring, loosen some soil in the row or raised bed that you are going to use. Place some of the soil into a waterproof container so that the depth of the soil is slightly more than the length of the two probes on your pH tester. (Read the instructions for your individual tester as some do vary.)

Now thoroughly moisten the soil, not too wet just enough to make the soil damp all the way through. This will allow the electronic probes to measure the conductivity in the soil. If it is too wet all that it will measure is the conductivity of the water. It is best to use pure water, such as you get in a water bottle. Spring water is not always pure, distilled water is best, but any brand of bottled water is better than most tap water.

As soon as the mixture is ready insert the probes their full length into the soil. Wait a minute or so and then check the pH reading on the scale.

How to correct the temperature and the pH of the soil.

You now have the two measurements that will determine whether you can plant or sow your seeds. If the soil temperature and pH are both within the ranges required you can go ahead and plant those seedlings and sow the seeds.

Increasing the soil temperature.

Sometimes the weather does not cooperate and the temperature of the soil is too cold. You can wait until the weather warms the soil or you can use one or all of the following methods to get the soil warm enough.

Laying a sheet of plastic on the raised bed or along the row is probably the quickest way to increase the soil temperature. I use black plastic as I get it for free from the local sawmill. I have used clear plastic and it heats up soil just as quickly as black. Make sure the edges are weighted down with stones or soil so that the plastic does not blow away.

A few layers of garden fleece helps to increase the temperature. Hold this down with stones or soil round the edges.

Another way is to mulch the soil with manure, compost or peat-moss. The mulch should be about 3 inches (7 ½ cm) thick.

A tunnel of clear plastic over the raised bed or row will also heat the soil.

Take the temperature daily and transplant your vegetables when the temperature reaches the required minimum for that crop, and stays at or above that temperature for at least 48 hours.

Adjusting the pH of the soil

The pH of the soil can be higher or lower than the required 6.4 to 6.9 and there are different ways of correcting this. In fact the pH gets slightly more acid each year, by about half a point.

If the pH is too high you add sulfur and if it is too low you add limestone. That is the simplest and quickest way, but garden soil containing lots of organic matter can adjust itself as the microbes in the soil will create a balanced environment for themselves which suits most of the plants that we grow.

As a bonus you will find that you will be growing more abundant and healthier crops and fewer weeds will grow in the healthy soil. Plus less bugs and diseases will be attracted to any sickly or weak plants, as your garden will only have strong healthy ones.

How much sulfur or limestone do you need?

As the pH scale is logarithmic (which means that a reading of 5.9 is ten times more acid than a reading of 6.9) if you wish to change the pH of your soil by 2 points that means you will have to increase or decrease the acidity or alkalinity by a hundred times!

I would not even try to do this. Adjust the pH 1 point up or down every year and add lots of organic matter to the soil as this will have a buffer effect against any potential problems. Your soil will very soon be in the right pH range for most plants and you can actually adjust the pH of different beds or rows to suit different crops.

Applying Sulfur

Elemental sulfur is the type you need. Also called "Flowers of Sulfur" (Sulphur is the spelling in the UK).It comes in the form of powder and should be very thoroughly mixed into the top 6 inches (15cm) of the soil otherwise you will have some areas that are more or less acid than others. To get an even covering use a lawn fertiliser spreader. Use gloves and a mask when you spread the sulfur powder.

The following weights of Sulfur will lower the pH of your soil by 1 point for an area that covers 100 square feet (9.3 square metres) of your garden.

Sandy Soil

1.75 lbs (790 gm)

Loam Soil

2.4 lbs. (1.088 km)

Clay Soil

3.6 lbs. (1.6 gm)

Applying Limestone

There are 3 types of limestone that are applied to gardens to adjust the pH so that the soil is less acid.

Dolomitic Limestone contains magnesium and calcium. Both are very important for optimum plant growth. If you are starting a new garden I would recommend that you get your soil tested before you plant anything and another test at least every 3 years thereafter. You will get better crops and you will also save money on fertiliser.

If your soil is shown to be lacking in magnesium then Dolomitic Limestone is the one you should put on your garden.

Pulverized Limestone is the type that is commonly used. It is less expensive but quite dusty to apply.

You can buy Pulverized Limestone that has been pelletized. This is more expensive but is easier to use as it is less dusty.

The following weights of Limestone will raise the pH of your soil by 1 point for an area that covers 100 square feet (9.3 square metres) of your garden.

Sandy Soil
2.4 lbs (1.088 km)
Loam Soil
5.5 lbs (2.5 kg)
Clay Soil
8.5 lbs (3.85 kg)

Starting seeds and transplanting seedlings in the garden.

The weather is cooperating, the garden has been cleared of all debris, the soil is at the correct temperature, the pH adjusted and the organic fertilizer added. The soil has been forked over to incorporate the fertilizer plus the timing is now right to sow the first seeds in the garden and transplant some seedlings.

It is very important to harden-off the seedlings so that they do not suffer a shock when exposed to the cooler weather outside in the garden. Hardening-off is gradually increasing the time that the seedlings are put outside each day over a period of at least a week, preferably two weeks.

When putting them outside for the first time, put them in a shady spot that gives them protection from the wind and the direct sun.

Transplanting is best done in the late afternoon so that the tender seedlings do not get the hot sun on them. This way they will have all of the night and early morning to adjust to their new environment.

Just to make sure there are no problems I always cover the new seedlings and newly sown seeds with garden fleece for at least a week. This will protect them from the sun, the wind and birds.

Hint: With all transplants consider using Willow Root Booster as described in "Transplanting the Seedlings" in Part 1 of this book. You should notice a great improvement on your root crops, like carrots and parsnips. (Of course you do not transplant root crops!)

Here is my week by week plan for transplanting and starting seeds in the garden.

5 to 6 weeks before the last frost.

If all the conditions are right for starting seeds then the following varieties can be sown.

Carrots, lettuce, radishes, parsnips, spinach.

Follow the instructions on the seed packets, water the seeds in carefully and cover the soil with garden fleece. If the weather gets cooler erect a small plastic tunnel over the seed bed. You can cover the seed bed with black plastic, but, take extra care to check daily for any seedlings that have germinated and to take the plastic off when any seedlings emerge.

Hint: Parsnips are renowned for taking a long time to germinate so interplant the parsnips with radish seed. The radish is very quick to grow and will protect the parsnips and be harvested before they emerge.

(Do not transplant any seedlings into the garden yet.)

4-5 weeks before the last frost.

The following seeds can be safely started now:

Broad Beans (Fava Beans), onions (sets and transplants), peas, turnips.

Hints: Onion transplants can normally survive without hardening off, but if needed I always cover them, just in case.

Peas and beans will germinate quicker if they soaked in water before sowing. Soak beans for one hour and peas overnight. I add one tablespoon of kelp-meal to each liter (pint) of water. This seems to give the plants a boost when they emerge from the soil.

When you are ready to plant the bean and pea seeds the plants themselves and your garden will benefit if they are covered with an inoculant. The inoculant encourages legumes (members of the pea and bean families) to fix nitrogen in the soil through the nodules that are growing on their roots. There are different inoculants for different legumes so make sure that you purchase the correct one for your beans and peas.

Broad beans attract black flies like bears to honey. So when they have 4 clusters of flowers cut off the tip of each plant.

This is the time to start hardening off broccoli, cabbage and kale seedlings.

3-4 weeks before the last frost.

Hardened –off transplants of broccoli, cabbage and kale can be set out in the garden.

Beets and seed potatoes can be sown now, plus a second planting of **spinach, carrots, lettuce, parsnips and radishes.** Continue to do this succession planting every 2 weeks until early summer. You will be harvesting a continuous crop of delicious young and tender plants instead of picking an enormous amount all at once.

Avoid having Beets growing near Mustard or Pole Beans as all three of these plants can be stunted if grown together. Beets grow best in firm soil. To firm up the soil tread carefully along the row or tamp it down with the flat end of a hoe after sowing the seeds.

2-3 weeks before the last frost.

Lettuce seedlings can be transplanted now if they are hardened-off.

You can also sow a mixture of salad mix (Mesclun). For a continuous crop all summer sow again every 10 days.

Start to harden off the more tender plants such as cucumbers and summer squash.

Frost free days (hopefully)

Transplant cucumbers and summer squash, but, have the garden fleece or even old sheets handy as Mother Nature does not always know the date of the last frost.

Start to harden off transplants of celery, tomatoes, peppers, winter squash and pumpkins.

1-2 weeks after the last frost.

Set out transplants of tomatoes, peppers, pumpkins, celery and winter squash.

When the soil is warm enough sow your other less hardy beans and more peas. If you have enough room and the family to eat them continue with your succession crops for as long as possible.

Hints:

An inexpensive way to protect plants from frosts is to cover them with a 1 gallon plastic milk jug that has the bottom cut away.

Young tender plants are a feast waiting to happen for cutworms. These are the larvae of moths that lay eggs in the soil and when the larvae emerge they head straight for the stems of newly planted seedlings.

There are several ways to thwart their efforts. One is to go round in the evening with a flashlight and hand pick the ones you see on your plants and destroy them. Another way is to encircle the stems with diatomaceous earth. Diatomaceous earth is made from the fossilized remains of aquatic organisms called diatoms. Their skeletons are made of a natural substance called silica which is extremely sharp. This silica penetrates their bodies when they crawl over it. The best way, in my opinion, is to stop the cutworms from getting to the plants by providing each plant with a cardboard collar.

I make mine from the cardboard rolls that are inside toilet and kitchen rolls. A four inch (10 cm) piece will push into the soil around the stem and protect it until the cardboard rots. By then the danger will be over and the larvae will be moths. They lay eggs in long grass and weeds, so mow regularly near the garden and weed the rows as often as you can.

CONCLUSION

Thank you very much for taking the trouble to read this first book in the Cariboo Gardener Series.

In the beginning of the book I promised to give "Step by step instructions to enable any gardener to confidently produce strong, organic vegetable seedlings that will grow into healthy, nourishing food."

I sincerely hope that I have helped you plan your organic garden, choose the seeds and to get them started at the right times and in the right conditions. Your seeds will now have grown indoors into healthy strong plants and these plants are now growing in your garden,

The garden has been fertilized so that the new seeds you sow outside and the transplants will all grow into the tasty nutritious food that I promised.

I know that any gardener who takes the trouble to get more knowledge will grow the best crops possible. I hope that you have wonderful results from your garden and that you will pass on your knowledge to other gardeners who need your help.

This series of gardening books is my way of paying back all the people who have helped me in my career in horticulture.

Would you please do me and the other gardening readers a great favor? For all authors and readers of books on Amazon the reviews of books help everyone. The prospective readers are helped in their decision to purchase and authors can learn a lot from the comments.

If you have enjoyed this book, and perhaps learned some interesting facts about organic gardening and seed starting, would you leave an honest review about my book Starting Seeds Successfully?

If you would like to be informed when the second book in this series is published you can visit my website at www.cariboogardener.com/ where you can also ask any question about organic gardening, which I will try to answer personally.

RESOURCES

SEED COMPANIES that sell HEIRLOOM and HERITAGE SEEDS.

This is not a complete list but includes companies that I have dealt with personally and some companies that fellow organic gardeners recommend.

Canada

https://www.heritageharvestseed.com

www.cottagegardener.com

www.saltspringseeds.com

https://www.westcoastseeds.com

www.hawthornfarm.ca

www.terraedibles.ca

www.veseys.com

USA.

http://www.rareseeds.com/

http://www.underwoodgardens.com/

www.victoryseeds.com/

http://heirloomseeds.com/

http://www.burpee.com

List of companies that are Monsanto free

http://in5d.com/list-of-monsanto-free-seed-companies/

Australia

https://www.edenseeds.com.au

www.greenpatchseeds.com

www.heirloomseeds.com.au

https://www.diggers.com.au

UK

www.realseeds.co.uk

There is a good list here!

http://www.radnor-raised-beds.co.uk/heirloom-seed-companies-uk-and-ireland/

Article about Monsanto buying seed companies

www.permaculture.co.uk/articles/monsanto-buys-heirloom-seed-suppliers

I buy my seeds for my Fall Fair entries from W. Robinson and Son – their website is-

www.mammothonion.co.uk

This following supplier is really good with the best selection I have seen.

Baker creek heirloom Seeds

www.rareseeds.com

SOIL TESTING and ORGANIC FERTILIZERS

Link to list of Canadian and USA soil testing companies.

http://www.agf.gov.bc.ca/faq/

Australia - soil testing Companies

www.csbp-fertilisers.com.au/csbp-lab

www.apal.com.au/services/soil-testing

www.coffey.com/en/our-work/services/testing-services/

www.sesl.com.au/

www.dpi.nsw.gov.au/aboutus/services/das/soils

www.agvita.com.au/

www.hitechag.com.au/Soil_plant_testing.aspx

Link to Penhallagon's "Values of Organic fertilizers"
http://extension.oregonstate.edu/gardening/node/955
Link to creating ideal organic Soil
http://www.soilminerals.com/Ideal_Soil_Main_Page.htm
Link to Organic Research Centre
http://www.organicresearchcentre.com/manage/authinclud
es/article_uploads/iota/technical-leaflets/soil-analysis-and-
management.pdf
Link to sample organic soil test
http://www.soilminerals.com/samplereportI.htm
This list is available on my website at----
www.cariboogardener.com/resources

ABOUT THE AUTHOR

Ken Bourne has been a professional organic gardener and nurseryman for over 50 years. He has owned two nurseries, a garden center and two florist's shops in Sussex, England, and also operated a landscaping business. He was one of the founding directors of the first company in the UK to sell packs of mushrooms that could be grown at home.

Chosen from worldwide applicants he managed and operated a 5 hectare greenhouse operation in Abu Dhabi in the United Arab Emirates where he grew tomatoes and cucumbers in the desert.

In 1982 he immigrated to British Columbia, Canada where he started and operated a greenhouse operation in the Cariboo region of that province. For almost 20 years he was the gardening correspondent for 2 local newspapers and also wrote gardening articles for other publications, including the well-known magazine Gardens West.

He still operates the nursery, although on a smaller scale, where he teaches gardeners about the benefits of organic gardening and gives talks on the making and use of compost and the addition of bio-char as a soil conditioner.

If you have any questions about organic gardening or gardening in general he would be happy to try and answer them.

His email address is:-

plantmanken@xplornet.ca

Or visit his website at

www.cariboogardener.com/questions